Horses

Horses

Explore the beauty of these majestic animals

Bath • New York • Singapore • Hong Kong • Cologne • Delhi
Melbourne • Amsterdam • Johannesburg • Auckland • Shenzhen

First published by Parragon in 2010

Parragon
Queen Street House
4 Queen Street
Bath BA1 1HE, UK

Designed, produced and packaged by
Stonecastle Graphics Limited

Designed by Sue Pressley and Paul Turner
Edited by Philip de Ste. Croix

ISBN 978-1-4454-2004-2

Printed in China

Page one: A magnificent white stallion shows off his paces.

Page two: The Trakehner is a warmblood breed often trained
to perform highly skilled movements in the dressage arena.

Page three: A handsome Hanoverian horse gallops freely
across a summer meadow.

Right: A small herd of horses graze peacefully on the shores
of a crystal clear lake in Russia.

Contents

Introduction

The horse has been an integral part of our lives for thousands of years, and it is all too easy to forget that it is, essentially, a wild animal. We are so accustomed to his domesticity – from riding school hacks to top class show jumpers and racehorses – that we often forget that there are still some places in the world where horses live wild or semi-wild in remote locations where the rules of 'survival of the fittest' prevail and conditions are often harsh.

No other animal has lived so close to humans, nor captivated us for so long – his destiny has always been linked with that of humans. The horse is part of our lives because of his generous nature, not just our coercion. From his early domestication, he has gone with us unquestioningly to war, became our foremost mode of transport, and remains our companion in sport and leisure. Mankind has enjoyed a unique relationship with the horse which has provided such intelligent, loyal service in so many ways and in modern times, the horse has even given rise to an entire industry from which many people make a living.

Differences in terrain, climate and man's requirements have shaped and developed the wide variety of types and breeds of horse and pony existing today – from the tiny Shetland pony to the massive and powerful Shire horse. Throughout history we have radically changed the lives of our horses to suit our own purposes and the horse has offered humans his strength and loyalty, and in return, we have bestowed upon him a status which is perhaps above that of all animals.

But despite centuries of domestication, horses still retain their independent character and it is a joy and a privilege to observe their natural behaviour – to watch them frolic and play, and kick up their heels with the sheer exuberance of living.

Right: Wild horses will instinctively form herds, usually comprising family groups of a stallion and five or six mares with their offspring. They will all sleep, play and feed together while constantly being alert to possible danger.

Running Free

Left: *From a very early age, foals run and play to build up stamina and strong muscles. Living in the wild, a foal would have to be able to keep up with its mother and the rest of the herd if there was danger.*

Below: *For survival in the wild, the horse depends on the 'flight or fight' mechanism – in a split second he has to decide if he will stand and fight a predator with his teeth and hooves, or gallop as fast as he can to avoid danger.*

Opposite: *From a standing start, a horse can reach a top sprint speed of more than 70 kilometres per hour (45 miles per hour) in three or four seconds.*

Opposite: *The Friesian is one of Europe's oldest breeds. It has been developed over centuries to create a horse with an extravagant action which combines natural strength, speed and stamina.*

Above: *With a willing nature and an impressive high-stepping trot, the Friesian is much-prized in many disciplines including carriage driving and dressage.*

Above and right: Horses love to run and play – sprinting at speed before turning tightly, bucking, kicking and snorting in the air. Their behaviour is motivated by instincts acquired during millions of years of natural evolution and the need to escape from predators.

Opposite and following pages: The horse is naturally a highly-strung animal whose instinctive reaction to danger is flight. This mechanism is clearly seen in the exuberant behaviour of domesticated horses when they play.

Left and above: The Shire horse (left), a heavy draught breed, and the Hanoverian (above) which today enjoys an excellent reputation in dressage and show jumping disciplines, both share the same basic characteristics as shown by their lively reaction to the exciting arrival of snow.

Opposite: The herd's social structure ensures constant vigilance and comparative security for each individual. Evolution has established that there is safety in numbers as a predator is likely to be confused by a group of animals galloping around.

This page: Safety for the wild horse is aided by a combination of excellent physical and sensory attributes – explosive speed and stamina to outrun a predator, as well as superb vision and hearing to detect any threat. These abilities are present in every horse and pony and many of today's numerous breeds have been specifically developed by man to exploit these natural characteristics.

Opposite: The herding instinct is very strong in all horses. These youngsters have been weaned from their mothers and turned out in the snow together where they instinctively form a small herd which offers security, companionship and fun for each member of the group.

Above: Breeds such as this striking Arabian have long been domesticated by man who continues to enjoy not only the breed's unique beauty but its intelligence, speed and agility.

Left: This strong, well-developed foal is capable of keeping up with his mother at great speed. In the wild it is important that a foal is standing within an hour of birth and soon after he should be able to walk and feed. Shortly after that he should be able to canter and call out to his mother, particularly if danger arises and the herd has to run away for safety.

The Beautiful Horse

This page: *Horse breeds can be identified by their ancestry. This fine Arabian (below) is the original hotblood of the world's horses, while the impressive Shire (right) descends from heavier, more primitive coldblooded types.*

Opposite: *Continued selective breeding has resulted in many warmblooded breeds which combine characteristics from both cold- and hotblooded ancestors.*

Above: *Man's influence on the horse has resulted in the creation of many different breeds which have each been developed with talents for particular sports and tasks.*

Left: *The combination of finer, faster hotblooded Arab or Thoroughbred lines with stronger coldblooded breeds has produced warmbloods which prevail in many equestrian sports including show jumping, eventing and dressage.*

Opposite: *The Fell pony is a traditional working breed which is often crossed with lighter breeds to create competition animals.*

Above: *This cheeky Exmoor pony exhibits the breed's characteristic prominent eyes, mealy-coloured muzzle and wide nostrils. The oldest of Britain's mountain and moorland breeds, it is a strong, hardy and intelligent pony which retains distinct features of the very earliest of original pony types.*

Left: *This handsome miniature Appaloosa pony has been selectively bred to produce this striking spotted coat.*

Opposite: *Selective breeding, often using Thoroughbred or Arabian bloodlines, has resulted in many fine riding pony breed*

Above: *Thought to be one of the oldest of all horse breeds, the elegant Akhal-Teke is a tough hotblooded breed which originated in the deserts of Turkmenistan. Today it is bred mainly for racing and is renowned for its endurance qualities.*

Left: *The Arabian has a few notable differences from other breeds, including the 'jibbah' which is the shield-shaped bulge extending between the huge, wide-set eyes upwards to a point between the ears and down across the top third of the nasal bone. It is this that gives the Arabian's profile a convex appearance.*

Above: Many hot- and coldblooded breeds have contributed to the warmblood over the centuries. Its development began when breeders aimed to produce a horse that could be worked on the land and used as a carriage horse and cavalry mount.

Right: Today, modern warmbloods such as the Oldenburg, the Trakehner and the Holstein are large, correctly proportioned riding horses combining elastic paces with good looks and an amenable temperament. They are in great demand as competition horses and virtually dominate the dressage arena.

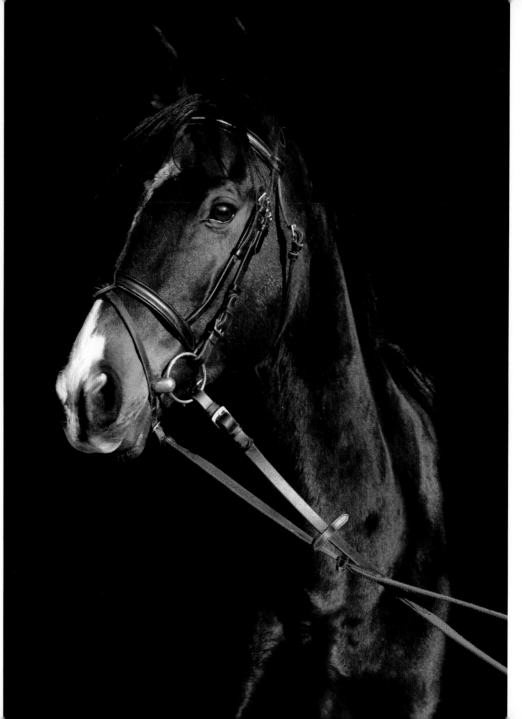

Manes and tails: *Nature's protection against the elements, manes and tails help to wick water away from eyes and other vulnerable parts in wet weather and shield eyes from the heat and bright sun in the summer. Tails and manes are also valuable fly swats and often two horses may be seen standing head to tail swishing their tails to keep the flies away from each other's faces. The manes and tails of domesticated horses are often trimmed to keep them clean and tidy and may be plaited for shows (left and below). This Fjord pony's mane has been cut to accentuate its ancient dorsal stripe (right). It is acceptable for some breeds to have their manes cut very short or 'hogged' (opposite).*

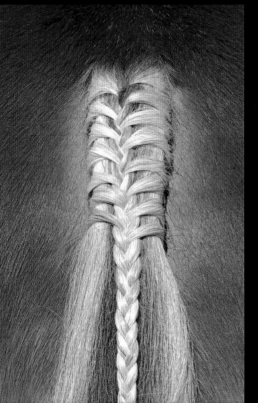

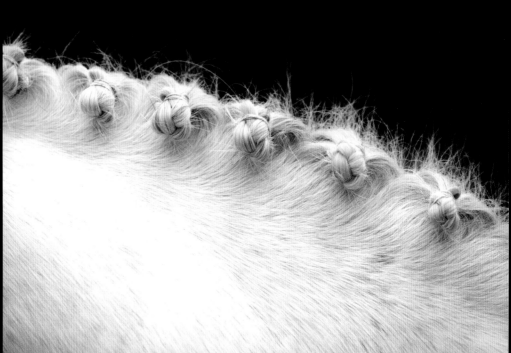

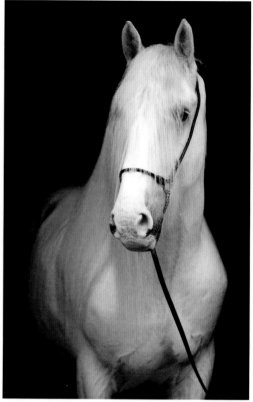

Above: *The magnificent Shire is Britain's best-known heavy horse breed and dates back to the 1700s. Familiar figures today at agricultural shows, these gentle giants stand up to 18hh and were developed as draught horses and to work the land – pulling ploughs and helping to haul felled trees from forests. The breed declined after the Second World War, but some are now once again being used by breweries and in agriculture and forestry.*

Left: *At around 14hh the handsome Haflinger pony is extremely strong for its size. The original tough native pony was crossed with Arabian blood resulting in a very versatile, intelligent breed.*

Above: *The Friesian is a stocky coldblooded draught horse thought to date back as far as 1000 BC. Although not a large animal, he was acknowledged by the Romans as being a superlative work horse, and was also highly valued as a knight's charger. Since then, the infusion of Spanish blood has created a finer horse which is extremely versatile. The breed is known for its handsome looks, endearing temperament and spectacular paces.*

Left: *The purity of the Arabian breed is strictly maintained by its own breed society, and Arab bloodlines have significantly influenced many other breeds over the centuries.*

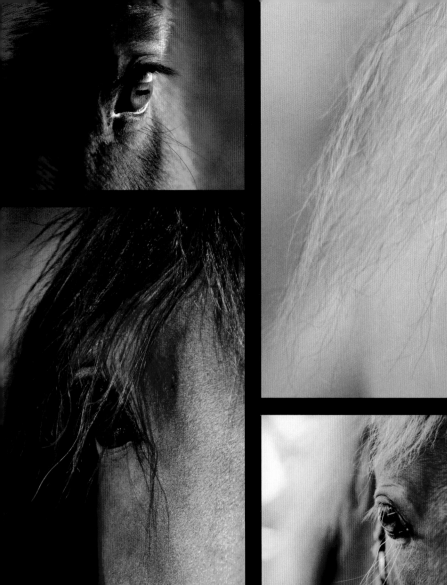

Eyes: The horse's large eyes, set either side of the head, provide almost all-round vision, essential for a prey animal that has to rely on its quick reactions and speed to escape predators. Unlike humans and other animals, the horse focuses on object by raising and lowering its head rather than altering the shape of the eye's lens. Although lateral vision is good, frontal vision is poorer and this should always be appreciated when riding or driving a horse or pony. It is said that the horse's eyes reveal the animal's nature. A horse may be said to have 'a kind eye' which may indicate a placid and friendly outlook, or he may have 'wild eyes' which might suggest the opposite.

Living With Horses

Below: Many people who share their lives with horses will often speak of their horse or pony's unique character and strong individual personality. To them, he can be described as a 'person' for he is so much more than a possession, a pet, or simply a mere conveyance – he is a true and loyal friend.

Left: For many of the world's poorest communities, horses are still the only affordable means of transport. In both urban and rural locations they continue to supply over half of the world's agricultural power needs.

Opposite: Archaeological evidence suggests that horses were first ridden around 6000 years ago – approximately 500 years before the invention of the wheel. Today, leisure riding and equestrian sports are more popular than ever and the entire horse industry contributes significantly to the global economy.

These pages: The Mustang is a tough little horse familiar to everyone who has seen a Wild West movie. Descended from Spanish horses brought to the New World by the Spanish conquistadors in the sixteenth century, by 1900 it is estimated that there were two million feral horses roaming free on North America's Great Plains. They are of stocky build, varying from 13hh to 16hh and can be any colour, the most common being sorrel – a light chestnut shade – and bay, with skewbald, piebald, palomino, black and grey also being seen. Although naturally shy, Mustangs can be tamed and they are often used as 'cowponies' – for their speed and agility are renowned.

Following pages: The horse has many roles to play in his domesticated life with humans, from being used as a semi-wild 'bucking bronco' in rodeo sports (left) to executing precise movements in the more sedate art of dressage (right). These two activities could not be more dissimilar, but they each tap into the horse's natural actions and behaviour. The rodeo rider uses the horse's primitive instinct to rid himself of a predator on his back, while the dressage rider trains the horse to perform movements which have been developed from the natural actions which can be seen in all horses at liberty, when they are free to express themselves and interact with each other.

Home sweet home: *The natural environment for the wild horse is the wide open plains, but our domestication of the species means that it is often more convenient to stable our equine friends. This is one of the many ways in which we have radically changed the lives of our horses to suit our own purposes. But the horse is a very willing partner and most will easily adapt to the routine. Provided the stable is spacious, he is properly fed and cared for, is given adequate exercise and turned out in a paddock for part of the day with companions, he will come to love his stable and appreciate the soft bed, comfort and security it offers.*

Best of friends: *The vast majority of the horse population is kept for recreation, and spending time around horses in a controlled environment is great fun for children. Young people and ponies seem to have a natural affinity and most professional horsemen and women will affectionately recall that they spent a great deal of time with horses in their formative years. Not only is riding, grooming, mucking out the stables and generally caring for ponies good physical exercise, it gives a great sense of freedom, builds confidence and teaches balance and coordination. It is wonderful to have an equine friend with whom you can learn new skills and have lots of fun.*

Opposite: It is believed that organized horse racing first took place in ancient Greece, but as human nature is so competitive, it is likely that races between horse riders took place as soon as mankind learned to catch his mount and ride him. Horseracing became a professional sport in the eighteenth century and today the closely regulated selective breeding of highly prized racehorses for speed and stamina – particularly the Thoroughbred and the Arab – has given rise to a huge global industry.

Right: Polo is an ancient team game that is thought to have been played in Persia 2500 years ago. It is played around the world in various forms by teams of three or four riders using a mallet to hit a small ball. It is a very fast game which requires highly trained and skilled ponies. The ponies are usually a Thoroughbred cross using Quarter horse or Criollo blood, possessing stamina, agility, speed, balance and responsiveness.

Left: The United States are the world's leading harness-racing nation. Horses pull a two-wheeled cart called a sulkie and race in a specified gait over a course of a mile (1609m). Most harness races are for pacers where the legs move in lateral, rather than diagonal, pairs, but there are also races for conventional trotters which are more usually seen in Europe.

Following pages: Dressage exemplifies the training of the horse to an exceptionally high level (left). A dressage competition involves riding a set series of movements in a freestyle routine devised by the rider. Marks are awarded for each movement, overall style, technique and rider position as well as for the freedom, suppleness and obedience of the horse. Show jumping (right) is a popular equestrian sport conducted at amateur and professional levels. The object is for the horse and rider to complete a clear round without knocking down a fence. Some competitions are also judged on speed.

Family Life

Right: *Naturally gregarious, horses are herd animals and any group turned out into a field together will soon form a 'pecking order', or hierarchy. These youngsters seem a little nervous, but soon the bravest will step forward to investigate new experiences and the others will accept him as the leader.*

Below and opposite: *A large herd may be made up of a number of separate families, each with members of all ages.*

Opposite above: *The mare carries her foal for 11 months. Foals are usually born in the spring when the weather is milder and the grass is growing – factors which contribute to the well-being of both the mare and foal. As soon as the foal is standing, it is important that he has his first feed of his mother's milk. This is called colostrum and it contains essential antibodies that the baby needs to survive and which will be quickly absorbed by his gut. He should consume at least one litre (35 fl oz) of colostrum within six hours of birth.*

Opposite below: *It is rare for horses and ponies to give birth to more than a single foal, although it does sometimes happen. There is a high risk that two weak babies will be born, instead of one strong one. In the wild, twins rarely survive.*

Right: *The foal relies on his mother entirely for the first few weeks of life, staying close by her side and never straying too far. He will gradually become braver and more independent as he grows stronger and more confident.*

Above and top: During the first hour of a foal's life a process called imprinting will take place, ensuring that an unbreakable and irreversible bond is created between the mare and foal.

Opposite: The bond between mare and foal is incredibly strong, so much so that if they are separated accidentally, they will ignore all obstacles and injuries in their efforts to be reunited.

Right: As the foal grows, interaction with his peers is a vital part of his development. Turned out with other youngsters, foals will soon form friendships.

This page: *Born in the wild, it is imperative that foals stand immediately, albeit shakily, on their impossibly spindly legs, because the herd has no idea where the next threat, the next predator, is lying in wait to make a tasty meal of the newcomer. Despite centuries of domestication, horses still have this inherent instinct and the first thing a new mother will do is to nudge her reluctant offspring to his feet.*

Opposite: *It is a steep learning curve for the newborn. He should be standing within an hour of birth as nature intends the foal to be able to flee from danger at his mother's side.*

Above: *Foals are born all colours. The colour is determined by the dominant and recessive genes of his parents. Grey is known to be a dominant colour, followed by bay, brown and black. Chestnut is a recessive colour, so a chestnut stallion mated to a chestnut mare will always produce a chestnut foal, although it is entirely possible for a bay stallion and a bay mare to produce a chestnut foal if they both possess the recessive gene.*

Left: *This little foal is a Palomino. He will grow up to have a beautiful flaxen-coloured mane and tail. In the USA Palomino is registered as a breed, but elsewhere it is a colour description.*

Above: The delightful markings of this miniature pony foal are described as broken-coated or 'coloured'. Such markings in two colours (piebald) or three colours (skewbald) are becoming more and more popular in Britain and across Europe. In the USA the coloration is much admired and is described as 'Paint'. Nowhere else in the world is the Paint (formerly known as Pinto) designated a breed, rather than a colour.

Right: White markings are described with different terms according to their size and position. This foal has a white 'blaze' on his face and three white 'socks' which end below the knee.

These pages: *Herds of wild or semi-wild horses and ponies can still be found in various locations around the world leading lives very similar to those of their ancestors. Often conditions can be harsh, but in the spring when the grass is plentiful and the weather is kind, families can relax together and teach their new offspring about life in the herd, how to find food and water and how to survive possible dangers.*

Following pages: *It is an endorsement of the horse's forgiving and tractable nature that he has allowed us to change his way of life completely yet is still willing to do our bidding.*

Index